making hair jewels & accessories

GABRIELLE BYRNE

First published in Great Britain in 2008
A & C Black Publishers Limited
38 Soho Square
London W1D 3HB
www.acblack.com

ISBN: 978-0-7136-8739-2

CIP Catalogue records for this book are available from the British Library and the U.S. Library of Congress.

Book design: Sally Fullam
Cover design: Sutchinda Rangsi Thompson
Photography: Dan Byrne
Commissioning Editor: Susan James
Managing Editor: Sophie Page

Printed and bound in China

This book is produced using paper that is made from wood grown in managed, sustainable forests. It is natural, renewable
and recyclable. The logging and manufacturing processes conform to the environmental regulations of the country of origin.

The author and publisher cannot accept any liability for the use or misuse of any materials or equipment mentioned in this
book. Always read any product and equipment instructions and take any necessary precautions.

contents

acknowledgements

I would like to say thank you to my editor Susan James who, with adroit thinking and inspired versatility, quite literally made this book happen. Thank you also to my photographer, Dan Byrne, whose artistic creativity and photographic vision breathed life into every project on each page.

I would also like to thank Pippa and Verity for their artistry, inspiration and unconditional support. As well as these, at the risk of sounding like an Oscar acceptance speech, I would like to thank all my suppliers, especially P.J. Minerals, TiaraMaking.com, Crystal-Beads.co.uk and Jewel Mania, whose generosity made it possible for the materials in the projects to be of such a high quality.

introduction

Welcome to Making Hair Jewels and Accessories. Throughout history, people have always used accessories for their hair. From ancient civilisations like the Egyptians and Romans right through until the modern day, people have complemented their hair with some sort of adornment creating a powerful statement about whom they are and how they want to be perceived by others. Historically, hair adornments such as spikes, forks and combs reflected a person's social status – the more expensive the hair adornment, the more wealthy and higher social status they had. Nowadays however, accessories have replaced those adornments. These may no longer represent your wealth and social standing, but they still have an immediate impact on your entire image and style. A person's hairstyle is an important expression of who they are. It is the first thing you notice when you meet someone and many don't feel right unless they think their hair is perfect. Who, in the modern world, hasn't heard of a 'bad hair day'? That is why the hair accessories we use need to be exactly right in order to enhance our 'crowning glory' perfectly.

Accessories can be glamorous, chic, sophisticated, elegant, classy and discreet – the list is endless, but in this day and age where everything is mass produced, an accessory that you have created yourself and is unique to you will give you a sense of your own identity and individuality. The following twenty projects will give you a head start (no pun intended!) when it comes to expressing that individuality.

They have been designed so anyone can tackle them. No in-depth knowledge of jewellery making is needed and any technique that is used will be fully explained in the Techniques section. By following these instructions, you'll create beautiful, timeless hair accessories that will speak for themselves no matter where you go and, if you want, you'll learn that by tweaking the odd design and colour, you will develop stunning, individual creations to which the only limit is your own imagination.

getting
started

This chapter sets out the materials, tools and basic techniques you will need to complete all the projects in this book. You'll see that there isn't a lot of special equipment required and all the techniques are quick and easy to understand. It might be advisable, however, to practice a little with some of them using some bits of spare wire (e.g. making a loop) so you can do it perfectly for the finished project.

Tools & Equipment

You will probably have the majority of equipment used in this book around the house but there are a few tools you may have to buy. The main tools are:

 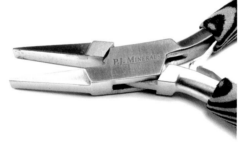 

∧ Round-nose pliers
Both jaws of these pliers are round so they are perfect for making loops with wire.

∧ Flat-nose pliers
Both jaws are flat and are used for gripping and crimping. Make sure both jaws are smooth on the inside as serrated edges, although good for gripping, will mark and damage your wire.

∧ Wire cutters
Used for cutting all plated and soft wire. A good quality pair of cutters will let you make a clean cut very close to your work.

The next two tools are optional but tend to make life just that little bit easier.

∨ **Nylon Jawed Flat nose Pliers**
These are extremely handy when using wire (especially when creating a spiral). These allow you to manipulate wire without marking it and straighten it out when mistakes have been made. They are also good for pressing wire components flat.

∨ **Electric Hot fix Applicator**
This tool makes gluing tiny crystals onto difficult places child's play.

tip *Superglue is great for its actual adhesive ability but be careful when sticking crystals because it tends to dull their shine, therefore I find it better to use epoxy resin.*

Apart from these items, you are quite likely to have most of the other necessary equipment around the house:

∧ Clockwise from top right hand corner: **Hole punch, Tweezers, Scissors, Beading needle** (the eye of sewing needles are too big to go through the holes in seed beads), **Paintbrush, Two-part epoxy resin glue, Ruler, Tape measure, Sandpaper/emery boards, Superglue**

Materials

As you might expect in a hair accessory book, you are going to need some hair accessories basics. Each project will outline what you actually need to make it but the following will show you the materials that have been used:

⌄ **Clockwise from top right hand corner: Barrette, Tiara bands, Hairpin (pick), Bendie clips, Hair comb, Concord Clip, Ponytail Holder**

Beads

The majority of projects use crystal beads or flatbacks and just out of personal preference, I tend to use Swarovski crystals because of their quality and brilliance. You can of course use any type of crystal that suits you.

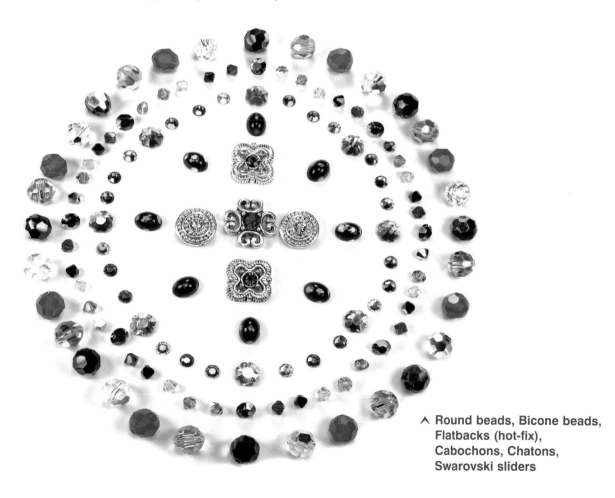

∧ **Round beads, Bicone beads, Flatbacks (hot-fix), Cabochons, Chatons, Swarovski sliders**

When using pearls, I have again opted for Swarovski because real pearls, apart from being absolutely gorgeous are, of course, quite costly and do not provide the uniformity of shape which enhances the look of the finished accessory.

Seed beads

Shell beads

Cloisonné beads

Wooden beads

Metal beads and spacers

Cats eye beads

Wire & Beading Thread

I have used both silver and gold plated wire that can be bought in measured spools and is flexible and ready to use. It is available in different sizes or gauges that can be a little confusing if you've not come across it before. A good base of rule is to remember that the higher the gauge number, the thinner the wire will be.

For the varying projects I have used:
0.4mm wire (28 gauge), which is more malleable for twisting
0.6mm wire (24 gauge)
0.8mm wire (20 gauge)

There are projects that require artists coloured wire as well, which comes in spools or on reels and measures, in the main, 0.6mm.

I have also used a thinner gauge beading wire for some projects (32 and 34 gauge) when I had to thread the wire through the same bead hole more than once.

Nymo beading thread is exceptionally strong and has the advantage of having a large range of colours.

Findings

Although findings are undoubtedly essential in all forms of jewellery making, you'll see that for the purposes of our projects, we'll only need a few – namely jump rings, head pins and a few bead caps and even then we won't necessarily be using them specifically for their original purpose.

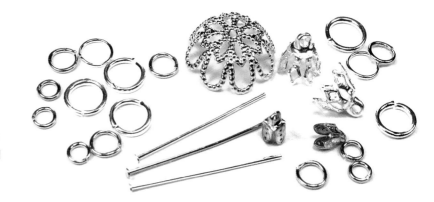

Miscellaneous

These items may seem quite ordinary but used in the right way; they can create the "wow" factor that we are all looking for!

Clockwise from top right hand corner:
Paint, diamond feathers, chains, clothes patch, chopsticks

Basic Techniques

The techniques outlined below have been used in various projects throughout the book. Each one has been numbered so you can easily refer back during the making of each project.

TECHNIQUE 1

Opening & Closing Jump rings

When you open jump rings, it is important to open them sideways with flat nose pliers so you don't distort the round shape.

Grip one side with your round nose pliers and the other with your flat nose pliers then gently twist your hands in opposite directions thereby 'opening' the ring.

To close a ring, again use the same technique with your pliers but as you twist the ends together, take the wire a little further than you need to so when you let go, the ends will automatically 'spring' shut and the ring will be more secure.

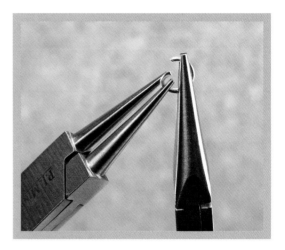

TECHNIQUE 2

Making Jump rings

Jump rings, of course, can be bought but knowing how to make jump rings is always useful if you ever

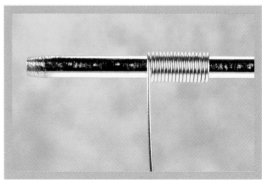

find that you don't quite have enough to finish a project or if you can't actually find the exact size you are looking for.

Find a hard cylindrical dowel that is the right diameter for the jump ring you want to make – this could be a knitting needle, a thick nail or any item that's lying around the house, which is the right shape.

Wind your wire around it as tightly as possible so you make a coiled spring on the dowel.

Take the spring off the dowel and, using your wire cutters, find the cut end and snip through to the coil above. This will make one jump ring. Carry on snipping until you reach the end of the spring.

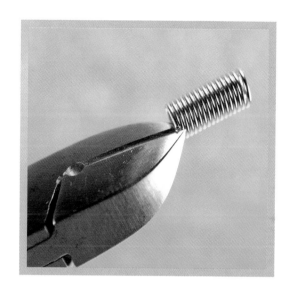

Finishing Ends

This technique is good for neatening off ends of wire and, also, for creating head pins.

Take the end of wire that needs finishing and grip the very end with your round nose pliers. Continue to curl the wire around the tip until you form a small hook.

To make a headpin, you can then take this hook and squeeze it flat with your flat nose pliers to create a small bump that will stop a bead from slipping off the wire.

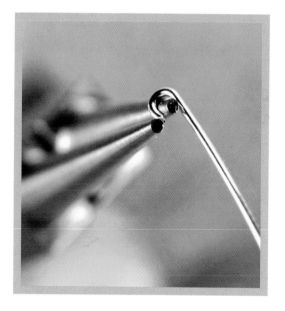

4 Making Spirals

Cut a length of wire and grip the tip with a pair of round nose pliers. Push the rest of the wire around the pliers with your fingers to form a tight circle. Try to make this as round as possible as the rest of the spiral will be formed around it.

Now hold this circle tightly in the flat-nose pliers and continue curling the wire around itself, making an ever-increasing circle. Nylon jawed pliers are good to use in this situation as they reduce marks made on the wire as you grip it, but are not essential.

For the purposes of this book, we need spirals that start off 'closed' (i.e. a tight coil) and end 'open' (i.e. with space around the spiral). This just means leaving a gap between the wire as you wind it round. This is harder because it is more difficult to create even gaps as you wind the wire but remember that this part of the wire will be hidden by your hair so don't worry too much if the circles aren't perfect.

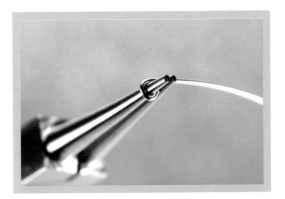

5

Making Loops

When attaching hanging beads to a project, the bead is going to need either a loop at one end or both ends depending on how you're going to use it. These loops need to be as neat and tidy as possible as they are generally on show in the finished article.

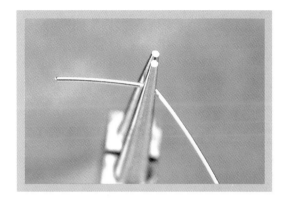

For a bead with a loop at each end take a length of wire – I find it best to thread the bead onto the wire, measure about 2cm on each side of the bead then cut this length with wirecutters.

Grip the wire about 2cm from the end with a pair of round nose pliers and whilst holding the longer end of wire, rotate the hand holding the pliers to an angle of about 60°. Without releasing the pliers, now use your spare thumb to bring the short end around the top jaw of the pliers. Take this as far as it will go.

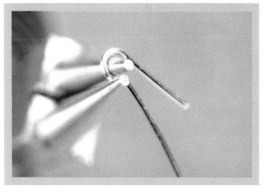

Now, release your grip of the pliers and rotate them so you still have one jaw inside the semi-formed loop and the other jaw above.

Grip the pliers again and bring the shorter end of wire under the lower jaw and across the other end of wire to complete the loop.

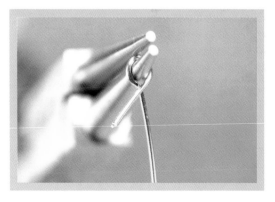

Neaten off the end with wire cutters by placing them inside the loop and cutting where the two wires cross. Please remember to cut the shorter end here and not the bit you're going to thread the bead onto.

Thread the bead onto the wire.

Make the loop on the other end in exactly the same way, except at the beginning bend the wire to around 60° where it touches the bead.

TECHNIQUE 6
Making Beads with Wire Twists

Make a bend in a piece of wire and thread a bead onto it.
Push this up to the bend.

Now, whilst holding the bead between your thumb and index finger and the two ends of wire in the other hand, gently twist the bead until the wire has a regular twist. (Be careful not to over-twist as this can make the wire snap.)

I have also used this method of twisting wire for the antennae of the butterfly in Project 10. The only difference is that you have no bead at the end to hold on to. Therefore, I find it easier to twist using pliers to steady the end instead.

TECHNIQUE 7
Making Crystal Sprays with Twisted Wire

Many tiaras, combs and hairgrips are adorned with beads using twisted wire, which gives them shape and form.

Once you know how to make a simple spray, you can experiment and go further to create flowers, more complex sprays, clusters and leaves to name but a few.

I have explained how to make a simple three-pointed spray for a tiara band, but you can attach it to any hair accessory such as a comb or pin.

Cut a length of wire approx 45cm long. It is usually best to use 0.4mm or 0.6mm wire as this is easier to manipulate than a thicker wire.

Near the centre of the tiara band, neatly wrap one end of the wire twice around the band so the end sits on the inside of the tiara.

As you might expect, the next bit is exactly the same as making beads with wire twists.

Make a bend in the wire about 5cm above the band and thread a bead onto the wire. Push this up to the bend. Now, whilst holding the bead between your thumb and index finger and the wire and band in the other hand, gently twist the bead until the wire has a regular twist up to the band. (Be careful not to over-twist as this can make the wire snap.)

Once you are happy with this twist, wrap the free end of the wire once around the band to anchor it.

Start the procedure again for the next crystal, only this time make the bend about 5.5cm above the band, thus ensuring this strand will be slightly taller than the first one.

Once you have twisted this wire, again anchor it by wrapping it around the band.

Now continue with the next bead. This is the same as the first one with the bend in the wire being about 5cm above the band.

Finish the spray by anchoring the wire to the band with a few more wraps and cut off any excess with the wire cutters.

You can make the bead any distance you like from the band/pin, just remember to make the bend slightly longer than you want the finished strand to be, as the wire becomes shorter the more you twist.

More Complex Sprays

Sometimes, you'll want to make sprays that branch out into more than one crystal on each strand. Although complex-looking, these are incredibly easy to make:

Once you have threaded the first bead, pinch the wire halfway down before twisting.

Take one end, bend again and once you have added another bead pinch the wires together and twist again.

Add more beads in this way and continue to create your spray. Finish by the twisting the ends of the wire together.

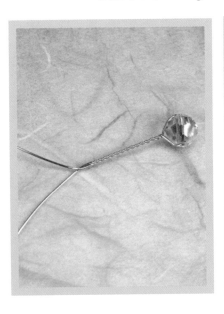 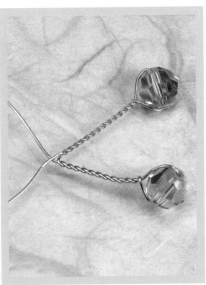 

Clusters & Flower Shapes

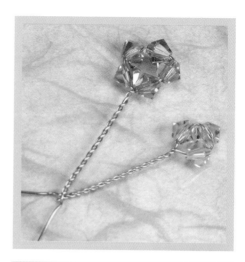

Simply adding more than one bead to each twist will make a cluster and will give a more solid appearance to your design.

The different number of beads you use will each create a different effect: e.g. a flower shape immediately springs to mind when five beads are added.

Bead Wrapping a Tiara Band/Comb

I find that once I've made a tiara or comb, the wrapped wire at the bottom can distract from the creation above, therefore I like to wrap beads across the band and so hide all the imperfections. This is a bit more fiddly but well worth it in the end. 4mm bicone beads are handy as they are approximately the same width as the band and fit snugly into each other as you wrap, but any sort of bead, such as pearls, also work very well.

Once you are happy with your design, measure out a long length of wire (about 50cm is probably the longest manageable length). Wrap this wire neatly round the band a few times, at about 5cm from the end of your

last spray, or, if you wish to decorate the whole band, start from the edge.

Thread a bicone onto the wire; position it on the front of the band. Hold it there while you wrap the wire around the back of the band and bring it to the front again.

Now thread another bead onto the wire and position it snugly against the first one, once again wrapping the wire around the back of the band.

Continue to wrap the band with beads across the whole length of your design. This can be a bit difficult in between the different twisted strands so don't try and rush it. If you run out of wire – don't panic! – just finish off by securing the wire a few times around the band and start a new piece off by wrapping the wire in between a few preceding beads so it is secure and then carry on with the beading.

Finish off by tightly wrapping the wire two or three more times around the band. Make sure no sharp bits of wire stick out.

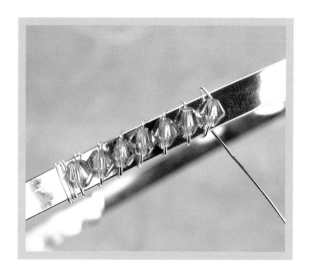

step-by-step
projects

set of six
hair jewels

It's the party of the year and everything's set – you've got a stunning outfit, shoes to die for, the make-up's perfect… but the hair isn't quite right… You need something to make you sparkle. That's why a dazzling set of hair jewels will complete the whole image of party superstar.

YOU WILL NEED

MATERIALS
6 x 15cm lengths of 1mm wire
6 x 6mm flat back crystals

TOOLS
Round Nose Pliers

Flat Nose Pliers
(Nylon jaw pliers are good if you have them)

Wire Cutters

Strong glue

step-by-step

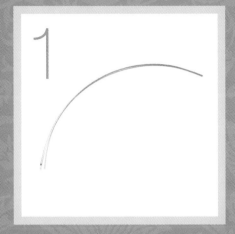

1

Cut a length of wire 15cm long.

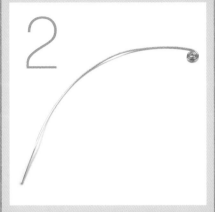

2

Create a closed spiral (see number 4 in Techniques section) large enough for the crystal to sit on.

3

Finish with an open spiral (see number 4 in Techniques section).

4

Curl the end of the wire (see number 3 in Techniques section).

5

Glue crystal to the centre of the spiral.

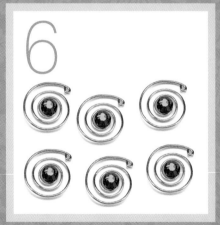

6

Repeat 5 more times.

step-by-step

1

Using your wire cutters cut the large rhinestone chain into 11 individual stones.

2

Cut the smaller rhinestone chain into the following lengths: 2 x 10 stones, 2 x 8 stones, 2 x 6 stones, 2 x 4 stones, 2 x 2 stones.

3

Measure to the centre of the clip and glue one large stone near the topside of the bar. Now take the two lengths of chain with 10 stones and glue either side of the larger stone.

4

Carry on by gluing two large stones on both sides of these lengths of chain and then take the eight stone lengths and secure them on either side. Continue in this way, again gluing two large stones on either side and then the six stone lengths.

5

Finally, secure the four stone lengths and two stone lengths, across the length of the clip, alternately gluing the large stones and then the smaller rhinestone chain to finish the cascade. Leave to dry completely.

PROJECT 2

This cascade clip combines style and sophistication with a little bit of bling thrown in for good measure. It's perfect if you want to add a little bit of magic to a long ponytail or if you want to spice up a shorter style – however you use it, it's sure to create the desired effect.

cascade clip

YOU WILL NEED

MATERIALS
8cm gold tone bar clip

10cm (approx) gold tone chain with sapphire blue 4mm rhinestone

30cm (approx) gold tone chain with light blue 2mm rhinestone

TOOLS
Wire cutters

Tape measure

Strong glue

step-by-step

1

Starting about 5mm from the top of the clip, glue a fuchsia crystal directly in the middle. This will be the top crystal of the first diamond shape. Now glue 2 more fuchsia crystals below the first one so a triangle is formed.

2

Carry on under these by gluing a fuchsia, a jonquil and then another fuchsia crystal to form a larger triangle.

3

Finish the diamond shape by securing two more fuchsia crystals under this and then one fuchsia crystal as the bottom point.

4

Leave a 2mm gap and then glue the next diamond shape to the clip by repeating the above process.

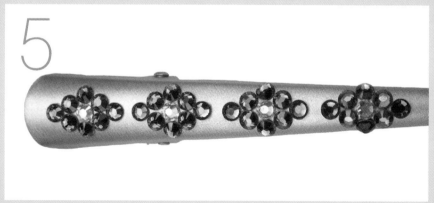

5

Continue down the clip until you have four diamond shapes.

metalic pink
concord clip

Going out but really haven't got time to spend hours on your hair? Then this party concord clip is the ideal solution. Gorgeous in it's own right, it's guaranteed to complete any look and only takes a matter of seconds to put in… just remember to let the glue dry before you use it!

YOU WILL NEED

MATERIALS
A 13cm metallic pink concord clip

32 x 4mm (ss16) round flatback fuchsia Swarovski crystals

4 x 4mm (ss16) round flatback jonquil Swarovski crystals

TOOLS
Strong glue

filigree barrette

This oval shaped barrette has a solid centre and a beautiful filigree pattern on the top and bottom that just shouts out to be decorated. This design somehow manages to be discreet and elegant while also grabbing the attention of all around. A wonderful show-stopper which lets everyone know you're there to be noticed.

With this project you are destined to become the Queen of any red carpet!

YOU WILL NEED

MATERIALS

1 plastic barrette with a filigree design

3 x 8mm x 6mm Swarovski AB crystal cabochons

125 x 3mm Swarovski AB crystal flower flatbacks (or enough to cover the design you have picked out)

TOOLS

Sand paper or emery boards

Pair of tweezers (optional)

Strong glue – epoxy resin is better than superglue here as superglue dulls the shine of silver backed crystals.

Sheet of paper

step-by-step

1 Pick out a design that you want to cover with crystals on the filigree barrette, and lightly sand these areas so the glue will stick the crystal and plastic together.

2 Place the barrette on the sheet of paper and working from the inside out, dab a small amount of glue on the back of the small crystals and, with the tweezers, place them on the pattern you have chosen. The sheet of paper will make it far easier to catch any small crystals that you drop.

3 Build your design with the smaller flatbacks and then leave to dry.

4 Attach the cabochons along the centre of the barrette and again leave to dry.

5 Once dry, gently tap the barrette against your worktop or your hand to make sure all the crystals are securely attached. If a few fall off – don't worry – just pick them up and re-glue, then leave to dry again. A filigree brass stamping or brooch front, attached to a large barrette with superglue or epoxy resin, would also work once you've picked out a design on the filigree to enhance with crystals.

aphrodite tiara

This tiara is named after the Greek goddess of love and beauty because that is who you'll feel like when you go out wearing it. The design can easily be made to complement whatever outfit you have just by changing the larger coloured crystals to a more suitable shade. Then all you have to do is accept the stunned admiration from all the lesser mortals who surround you.

Chic and glamorous are the bywords for this accessory yet it is incredibly easy to create.

YOU WILL NEED

MATERIALS
1 silver tone tiara band (this can be a plain band or one with small combs at each end for extra stability.)

0.4mm silver plated wire

9 x 5mm Siam red Swarovski crystal bicones

65 (approx) x 4mm clear AB Swarovski crystal bicones

TOOLS
Wire cutters

Round nose pliers

Flat nose pliers

Ruler

step-by-step

1 Create the central crystal spray. (See numbers 6 and 7 in Techniques section). Position this spray in the centre of the tiara band and make it more stable by gently pressing the wire wraps to the band with your flat nose pliers.

Try to ensure the ends of the wire are flat against the band at the back and will not hurt anyone wearing the tiara. If they stick out a bit, just press them back in with your pliers.

2 Now we can make the clear sprays which frame the central one.

Cut a piece of wire about 30cm long and, again, follow the crystal spray instructions (See numbers 6 and 7 in Techniques section) except make the bend in the wire about 2.5 cm above the band and use clear crystals.

Position these sprays on either side of the middle one.

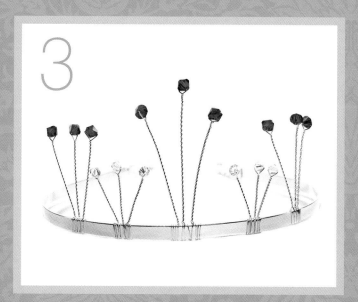

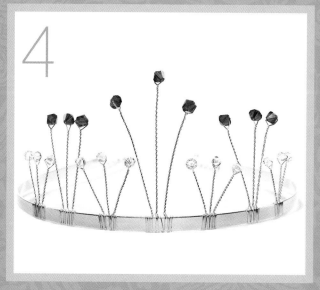

The next sprays on either side of the clear ones are using the red beads again. The technique is the same again, only this time you will need a piece of wire about 37cm long. Wrap the wire around the band and make a bend about 3.5cm above.

Now create two more clear sprays, the same size as the first clear sprays, and place them on either side of the red ones.

Wrap the band with clear beads (see number 8 in Techniques section). Arrange the sprays so they don't all uniformly stick straight up. By putting a slight curve into the strands, you'll get a more natural feel to the whole tiara.

daisy hair comb

This daisy hair comb brings with it a sense of understated glamour. It is fresh and natural but still has the effect of making people stop and take notice – so whether you need to keep control of long locks or if you just want a stunning accessory to finish off that perfect outfit, the daisy hair comb is the perfect solution. In this project, blue has been used as the main colour but of course this is easily substituted for any colour, which makes your comb unique to you.

YOU WILL NEED

MATERIALS

A clear plastic hair comb measuring approx. 8cm

5 x 5mm Swarovski light blue silver backed pointed chatons

70 x 5mm silver plated jump rings

107 x 3mm gold plated jump rings

TOOLS

Round nose pliers

Flat nose pliers

Strong glue (it is best to use epoxy resin to attach the chatons so the crystals do not appear dull)

1

Make the centre of the first daisy. Place two silver 5mm rings on top of each other and put 12 gold 3mm rings onto this pair of rings. (See number 1 in Techniques section.)

2

To make the first 'petal', put another pair of silver 5mm rings in two of the 3mm rings already set onto the centre, and before you close this pair of 5mm rings slip 4 more gold 3mm rings onto it.

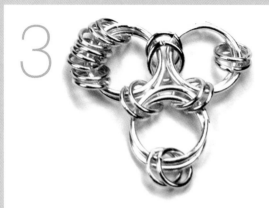

3

For the next 'petal', take another pair of silver 5mm rings and slip it through two 3mm rings from the first petal and another two 3mm rings off the centre ring. Before you close this pair, slip another two gold 3mm rings onto it. Continue like this all the way round until you have 6 petals.

4

The last pair of 5mm rings is attached to the centre by two 3mm rings and to the first 'petal' by the two smaller rings already in place.

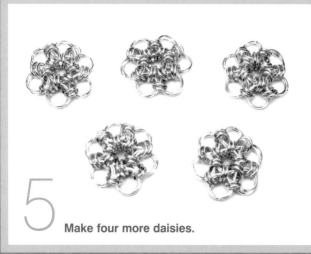

5

Make four more daisies.

6

Link the five daisies together in a chain by securing each daisy to the next with three gold coloured rings.

7

Glue a chaton into the centre ring of each daisy and leave to dry.

8

Take the completed chain of daisies and
secure them to the top of the comb with glue.

bohemian shell barrette

This barrette is ideal for that holiday look which screams casual yet exclusive. It's perfect to keep unruly tresses under control on the beach or for cutting a dash on a country estate golf course or there again you may like to wear it during that Mediterranean cruise down by the pool…

YOU WILL NEED

MATERIALS

1 silver tone barrette approx. 7cm long

8 x 25mm natural shell disc beads

4 x large silver-plated round spacer beads

Antique copper seed beads size 11/0 (approx. 3 grams)

10 x 4mm rose crystal bicone beads

10 x 4mm clear crystal bicone beads

10 x 4mm peridot crystal bicone beads

4 x 4mm silver-plated jump rings

Nymo white beading thread

TOOLS

Round nose pliers

Flat nose pliers

Scissors

Beading needle

Strong glue

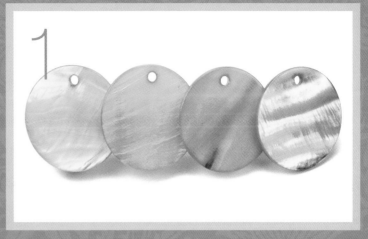

Glue 4 shell disc beads onto the barrette, slightly overlapping, so the hole of each bead is at the top. At the back, make sure there is enough bead showing below the barrette so you can glue the next row of shell beads.

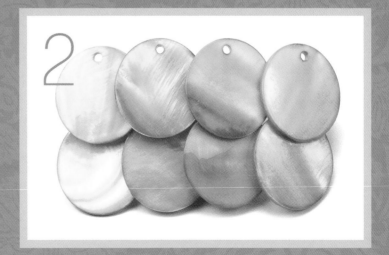

Now glue the next row of shell beads beneath the first row, again slightly overlapping each other. Make sure the holes are hidden by the first row.

step-by-step

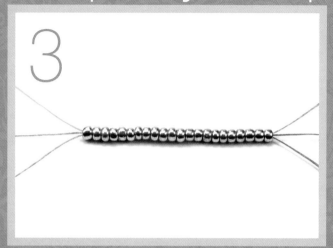

Thread the needle with approx 90cms of beading thread and pick up 22 seed beads so there is one strand running through the beads. Now take the needle back through the beads so you have three threads running through the beads.

   Make each of these three threads with the 22 seed beads roughly the same length of 30cms.

   Push the beads to the centre of the cotton and snip the thread at both ends so there are three separate threads.

Bend this 3-strand thread in half so you have 11 beads on each side of the bend and make a double knot under the beads. You should now have a loop of beads with six long strands of cotton.

Slip a spacer bead over all six strands and push up over the knot.

   Now thread one strand with the needle and randomly thread more copper seed beads and a crystal bicone so it measures just over 2cms from the spacer bead. Make sure the last bead on the strand is a seed bead that will act like an anchor, then, when you secure the thread, you can miss this last bead before taking the thread back through a number of seed beads and tying off.

6

Thread all six strands with seed beads, placing random crystals on each one.

7

Repeat this beading process three more times.

8

Now take the barrette with the shell discs and attach each beaded strand at the top of the loop to the shell beads with a jump ring (see number 1 in Techniques section).

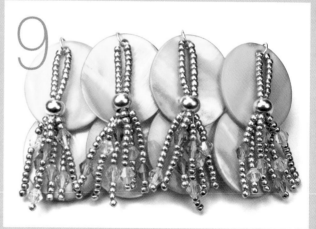

9

Secure each spacer bead with a dab of glue.

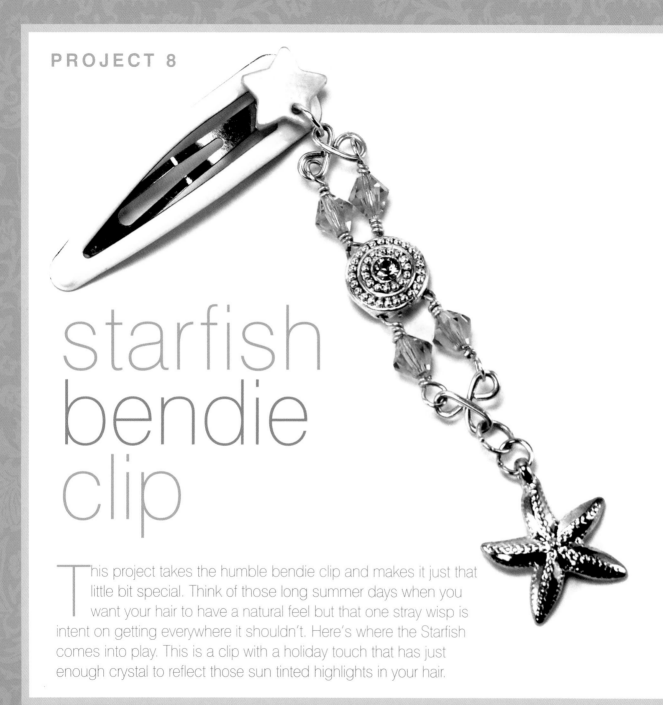

starfish
bendie
clip

This project takes the humble bendie clip and makes it just that little bit special. Think of those long summer days when you want your hair to have a natural feel but that one stray wisp is intent on getting everywhere it shouldn't. Here's where the Starfish comes into play. This is a clip with a holiday touch that has just enough crystal to reflect those sun tinted highlights in your hair.

YOU WILL NEED

MATERIALS

1 white bendie clip

1 x blue Mother of Pearl star shaped bead

1 x silver tone starfish charm

1 x round silver tone Swarovski slider with light blue crystal (4 holes)

4 x 6mm light blue Swarovski bicone crystal beads

7 x 4mm silver plated jump rings

0.6mm silver plated wire – approx. 20cm

0.8mm silver plated wire – approx. 15cm

TOOLS

Strong glue

Round nose pliers

Flat nose pliers

Wire cutters

step-by-step

1

Cut the 0.6mm wire into four equal lengths and make four double looped beads with the bicones (see number 5 in Techniques section).

2

Attach these to the Swarovski slider with 4 jump rings (see number 1 in Techniques section).

step-by-step

3

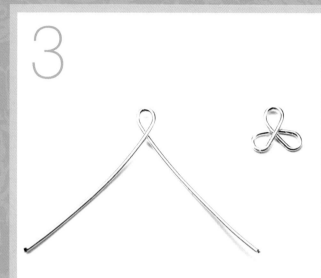

Cut the 0.8mm wire in half.

   With one half grasp the middle with round nose pliers and bend both sides right around, so the ends cross over each other

   Now take each end and using the round nose pliers again, curve each end up and around to make two more loops. Neaten off with wire cutters. You will now have a cloverleaf shape.

   Repeat the process with the other half of the 0.8mm wire.

4

Attach each cloverleaf to the two free loops of the bicone beads on each end of your dangle. Slightly open each loop in the same way as a jump ring and slip on the cloverleaf. Once attached, close the loop again.

5

Attach one end to the star shaped bead with a jump ring (see number 1 in Tecniques section).

Attach the starfish charm to the other end.

If your starfish charm doesn't already have a hanging ring put a jump ring on it before you add another ring, to attach it to the main body of the project.

6

Secure the back of the star shaped bead to the end of the bendie clip with strong glue.

jewelled
ponytail holder

It's holiday time and the last thing you want to do is spend hours on your hair but you still feel that a plain ponytail is letting the side down… just that little bit. This holder provides the perfect solution. In a matter of seconds you will have transformed your hair from something you want to cover up into a classy and sophisticated style you want to shout about instead.

YOU WILL NEED

MATERIALS
A black, plain oval ponytail holder and stick

3 x 15mm gold tone filigree bell caps

3 x 4mm fuchsia round Swarovski flatbacks

45 (approx.) x 3mm rose round Swarovski flatbacks

TOOLS
Strong glue

step-by-step

1 Glue one fuchsia flatback onto the centre of each of the bell caps.

2 Remove the stick from the holder and make it as flat as possible, now take the 3mm flatbacks and glue them around the outer edge. Ensure the crystals are evenly spaced and remember to leave a gap at either end where the stick is pushed in and out.

3 Now glue the bell caps onto the centre of the holder, evenly spaced, on a level with the end holes and in a straight line.

TO MAKE YOUR OWN HOLDER

MATERIALS

A large black heavy clothes patch approx. 10 x 10cm

A chopstick

A large wooden bead (with large hole)

Black paint

TOOLS

Superglue

Hacksaw

Pencil sharpener

Small paintbrush

1 Cut off the end of a chopstick so that it measures 13cm and glue on a large holed wooden bead. Leave to dry.

If the hole in your bead is slightly smaller than the chopstick then use a pencil sharpener to taper the end.

2 Take the large black clothes patch then fold and glue it in half to give a double thickness. Now cut out an oval measuring 9.5 x 5cm and hole punch it at each end.

Paint the stick and bead black. Leave to dry. Decorate as before.

Simple yet stunning, this butterfly pin will give your hair that lovely summer feel all the year round. I've given mine a purple twist in honour of the butterfly called the Purple Hairstreak but you can make yours a Cabbage White, a Red Admiral or an Adonis Blue – it's however the mood takes you.

butterfly
pin

step-by-step

YOU WILL NEED

MATERIALS

A large hair pin or pick

32 gauge silver tone beading wire approx. 40cms

4 x 4mm white Swarovski pearls

14 x 4mm Tanzanite Swarovski bicone beads

10 x 4mm Light Amethyst Swarovski bicone beads

TOOLS

Flat nose pliers

Round nose pliers

Wire cutters

Glue (optional)

Thread seven Tanzanite bicones and push them roughly to the centre of the beading wire. Now take one end and re-thread back through the first bead in order to make a loop. Do this again with the other end so the bottom wings of the butterfly are formed.

Hold both wire ends together and thread two pearls. Push these up to the bicones and then position the pearls and wire so they sit between the wings. These form the bottom half of the body.

Now fold the wire up behind the pearls so the ends are pointing up above the wings.

Make the top wings in the same way as the bottom. Thread 5 light amethyst bicones onto one wire and create a loop by threading the end back through the first bead. Do the same with the other wire end.

With both wire ends together bend the wires approx. 1.5cm from where they exit the light amethyst beads. Grip these 0.5cm from the beads with your flat nose pliers (so you have 4 wires in the pliers) Now, keeping your grip on the pliers, take one bend in the wire with your round nose pliers and twist (see number 6 in Techniques section) in order to make an antenna.

Maintain your grip on the flat nose pliers and repeat with the other bend.

Make sure both wire ends are at the front of the butterfly.

Thread two more pearls for the upper half of the body onto both wires together and push them up to bottom of the antennae.

Take each wire end between the upper and lower wings and behind the butterfly.

Twist them together for stability.

6

Attach the butterfly to the pin by wrapping each wire around the top of the prongs.

Neaten off the ends with wirecutters and press them onto the pin so they lie flat.

Wrapping the wire round the pin can be a bit tricky but don't worry too much about how neat it is as this is the side that no-one will see. The wires need to be quite tight and wrapped around both prongs of the pin at the top. Once wrapped, if your butterfly feels a bit wobbly, use your flat nose pliers and press the wires together on the pin and then, if you're still worried, drop a dab of glue on the back for extra security.

Turn the pin back over and arrange the antenna so they are slightly splayed apart.

orchid pin

Delicate and refined are just two of the words that spring to mind when you see this particular pin. Inspired by the weeping orchid, this flower will add a touch of oriental style to your look.

YOU WILL NEED

MATERIALS

A large hairpin or pick

4 x Marquise shaped light green shell beads

5 x 4mm silver tone bead caps

5 x 3mm silver plated plain round beads

9 x 4mm pink cats eye beads

6 x 4mm white Swarovski pearls

Strong pink beading thread (I like to use Nymo)

Silver-plated 32-gauge beading wire

TOOLS

Superglue

Beading needle

Flat nose pliers

Wire cutters

Scissors

step-by-step

1

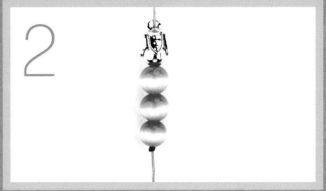

2

Attach the marquise beads to the pin with beading wire so they look like a backdrop of leaves. Thread each bead then wrap the wire several times round the top of the pin. Pull the wire tight and cut as close to the pin as you can. Press the end in with your flat nose pliers and make sure no sharp bits are sticking out. Secure with superglue if the leaves feel unstable.

For the flowers, thread the beading needle and make a double knot on the end. Now slide three cats eye beads onto the piece of Nymo cotton and up to the knot. Next thread a silver bead and top it with a silver bead cap.

3

4

Thread the end of the cotton through the bottom bead hole of the leaves attached to the pin and bring it through to the back. Attach this thread behind by wrapping it around one of the prongs of the pin and tying it. Again secure with a dab of glue if necessary. Neaten off both ends of the thread.

Make 4 more flowers in the same way using the cats eye beads and the pearls, and then attach them to the pin. In order for the pink ones to fall in the middle, place a white flower in the top left hole and a pink one in each of the remaining three. Then thread the extra white flower through the bottom right hole (that already has a pink flower) to give a framing effect.

63

starburst pin

With this pin everyone will know you've arrived. It has so many faceted crystals that it picks up and reflects any light, shimmering about your hair. Starburst? Perhaps we should have called this one Supernova!

YOU WILL NEED

MATERIALS
A large hairpin or pick

5 x 4mm AB clear round Swarovski crystal beads

5 x 4mm light rose round Swarovski crystal beads

10 x 5mm AB clear round Swarovski crystal beads

1 x 8mm light rose round Swarovski crystal bead

0.4mm gold plated wire

TOOLS
Flat nose pliers

Wire cutters

Superglue (optional)

step-by-step

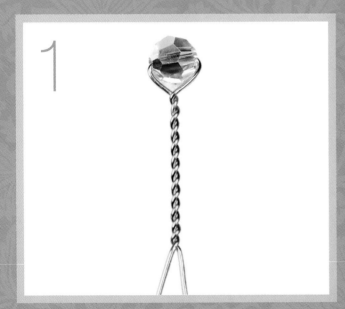

Take a length of approx. 50cm of wire and thread on a 4mm AB clear bead about 7cm along the wire.

Bend the wire so the bead is at the curve, pinch the two parallel ends approx. 1.5cm below and twist the wire (see number 6 in Techniques section).

Once this is twisted, thread on a light rose 4mm crystal onto the longer end of the wire, and again make a bend just under 1.5cm. Place the bead on the curve and repeat the above process.

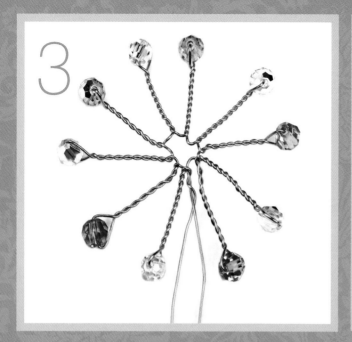

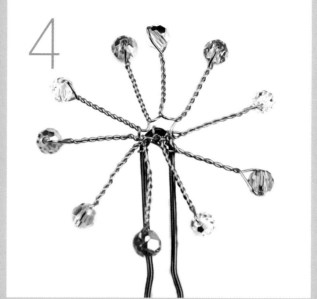

Carry on alternating all the 4mm beads in this fashion, then cross the two ends over so you have a circle of beads.

Wrap the ends of the wire tightly around the prongs of the pin at the top.
   Neaten off with the wire cutters and secure by pressing the wrap with the flat nose pliers.

Now take another length of wire approx. 40cm long and create another circle of beads with the 5mm beads using the same process, only this time make each bend approx 0.5cm along the wire.

6

Place this on top of the first circle of beads and take the two ends of wire past the twisted strands of the first and secure to the top of the pin in the same way.

7

Finally, thread the 8mm bead onto a piece of wire and placing it in the centre of the previous two circles now attached to the pin, secure it by taking the wires behind and wrapping them around the prongs.

Stabilise the wraps by pressing them with the flat nose pliers and if necessary dab with a little superglue to anchor firmly.

step-by-step

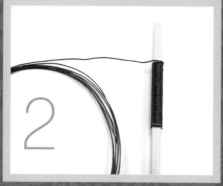

1 Cut a chopstick approx. 16 cm from bottom and sand the top so it is smooth to the touch.

2 Starting about 6 cm from top, wrap the pink wire tightly around the stick and work your way up to the top so that the upper half of the stick is completely covered. Try to keep the wrapping tight so no gaps form in the wire covering.
Once wrapped, cut the remaining wire off with wire cutters.

3 Cut 10 cm of gold chain and wrap it three times in a diagonal over the pink wire from the bottom to the top, making sure that the end chain link stands proud from the stick. Glue in place.

4 Thread a cloisonné bead onto a head pin and make a loop in the wire (see number 5 in Techniques section). Repeat 3 times.

5 Cut 3 more lengths of chain measuring 2cm, 3cm and 4cm. Attach a cloisonné bead (with a wire loop) to each length of cut chain with a jump ring (see number 1 in Techniques section).

6 Attach a jump ring to the end link of the chain glued to the stick and slip the three chains with the beads onto the same jump ring. Close the ring. Repeat procedure with other chopstick.

japanese
sticks

N o longer the prerogative of the ancient Geisha or the aristocratic French, this simple hair stick will turn your ordinary ponytail into a fantastic, beautiful style that will make heads turn wherever you go.

YOU WILL NEED

MATERIALS

1 pair of chopsticks

6.5m (approx) x 0.6mm deep pink coloured modelling wire

40cm (approx) gold coloured chain

6 x 6mm red cloisonné beads

8 x 4mm gold coloured jump rings

6 x gold coloured head pins

TOOLS

Strong glue

Hacksaw

Ruler

Sand paper or emery board

Round nose pliers

Flat nose pliers

Wire cutters

woodland tiara

Whether you want to be Titania, Shakespeare's Fairy Queen or maybe just have a 'one with nature' look, this Woodland Tiara clicks all the right buttons. The natural shades of pink, green and white blend together to form flowers, petals and leaves and ensure that the wearer will be the natural queen of all she surveys.

YOU WILL NEED

MATERIALS

A gold tone tiara base

0.4mm gold plated wire

3 x 8mm white Swarovski pearls

5 x 6mm white Swarovski pearl

16 x 4mm white Swarovski pearls

7 x 6mm light green bicone Swarovski crystal beads

4 x 5mm clear bicone Swarovski crystal beads

12 x 4mm clear bicone Swarovski crystal beads

3 x 6mm Crystal powder rose Swarovski pearls

66 (approx.) x 4mm Crystal powder rose Swarovski pearls

TOOLS

Round nose pliers

Flat nose pliers

Wire cutters

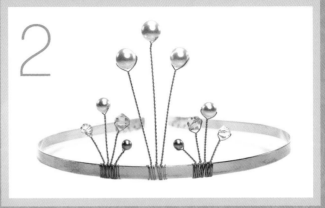

Start by creating a central spray of three 8mm white pearls (see number 7 in Techniques section) and position in the middle of the band.

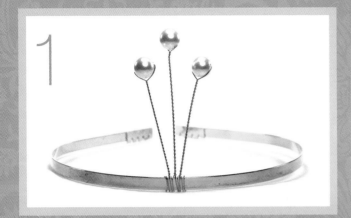

Now, keeping in mind there are going to be four sprays on either side of the central one to keep the tiara balanced, make the next two sprays and place them on either side of the large pearls. Don't necessarily keep to the same arrangement of beads used in the tiara shown but experiment if you want. Create a flower or two by threading five, three or two beads instead of one before you make a twist. Mix and match your sprays.

Continue making sprays until you have four on either side of the central one.

This next stage is optional but I find it completes the whole tiara and covers any unsightly wire wraps.

Wrap the tiara band with the crystal powder rose 4mm beads (see number 8 in Techniques section).

Be sure to cover the entire part of the tiara band that can be seen from the front when you are wearing it.

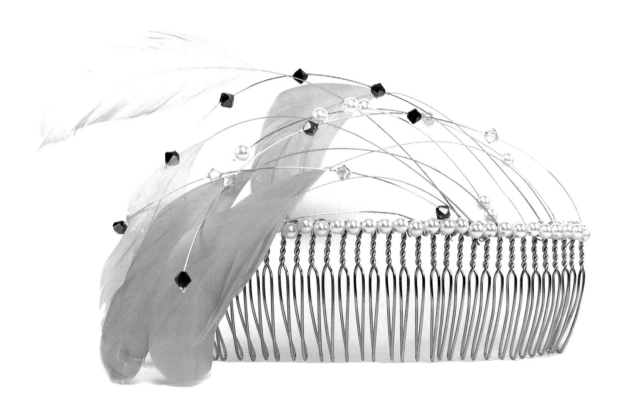

comet trail hair comb

Are you ready to stand out from the crowd? The Comet Trail Hair Comb is delicately enhanced with AB crystals that help to reflect the light onto the perfectly positioned pearls. The whole ensemble is finished off with a trailing backdrop of feathers. If you ever need to make an entrance then the Comet Trail Hair Comb is the one for you.

YOU WILL NEED

MATERIALS
A large silver tone hair comb

4 x 4mm silvershade bicone Swarovski crystal beads

4 x 4mm jet AB bicone Swarovski crystal beads

5 x 4mm crystal dorado bicone Swarovski crystal beads

45 x 4mm white Swarovski pearls

3 x silver diamond feathers

3 x almond diamond feathers

0.6mm silver plated wire

0.4mm silver plated wire

TOOLS
Round nose pliers

Flat nose pliers

Wire cutters

Strong glue

step-by-step

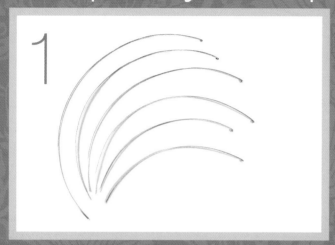

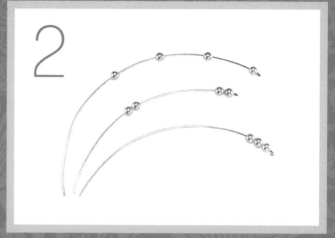

Leaving the natural curve in the 0.6mm wire as it comes off the spool cut the following lengths: 10cm x2, 13cm, 14cm, 15cm, 17cm. Create a head pin ending on each piece of wire. (See number 3 in Techniques section.)

Take a 10cm piece of wire and thread on three 4mm pearls. Push them to the end and secure with a dab of glue. Continue with the other 10cm length and thread on two pearls. Push them to the end and secure with glue. Now, approx. 4.5cm along the wire, thread on another two pearls and secure them in this position with adhesive.

Now take the 13cm length and adhere four single pearls at intervals of approx. 2cm.

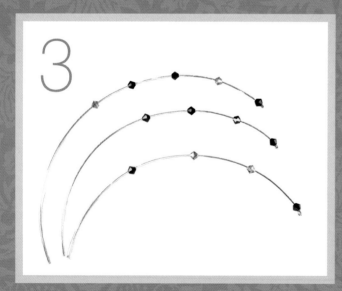

For the remaining wires, thread on the following combination of beads:

14cm length of wire – thread on and secure 1 crystal dorado bicone then 2 silvershade followed by another crystal dorado. Leave a 3cm gap between each bead.

15cm length of wire – thread on and secure 1 jet AB bicone then a crystal dorado, then another jet AB followed by another crystal dorado. Leave a 2cm gap between each bead.

17cm length of wire – thread on a jet AB bicone, then a silvershade, then a crystal dorado, followed by another jet AB and finish with a silvershade. Leave a 2cm gap between each bead.

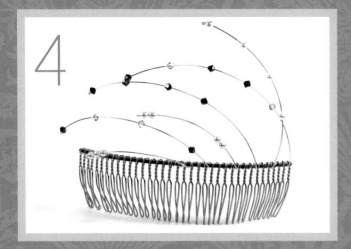

Measuring approx. 6-7cms from the right hand edge, place the wires on the comb in the following order:

The 10cm length (with the set of 3 pearls).

Then the 14cm length (with a crystal dorado, 2 silvershade and a crystal dorado).

Then the 10cm length (with the two sets of 2 pearls).

Then the 15cm length (Jet AB, crystal dorado, jet AB, crystal dorado).

Then the 13cm length (with the four single pearls).

And finally the 17cm length on the right hand edge .

Leave approx 1cm between each wire as you attach them to the comb.

Attach these beaded wires to the hair comb by taking each wire approximately 3cm from the end and wrapping it around the top of the comb until secure. Cut off any excess wire.

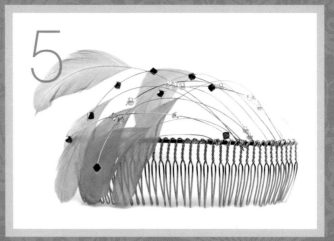

Attach the feathers with 0.4mm wire to the comb and place them in-between the beaded wires so they drape over the left hand side.

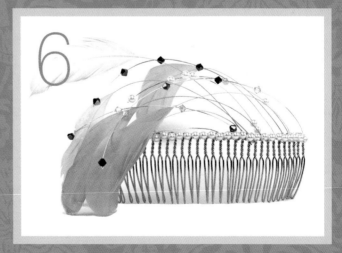

Bead wrap the hair comb with 4mm pearls (see number 8 in Techniques section).

Ensure the ends of the feathers are behind the beaded wires but in front of the hair comb

step-by-step

1

2

Place a flower on the band of the hair comb so a petal covers the edge and make a note of the place the hole covers. Now attach the wire here by wrapping the band a few times.

Thread the flower onto the wire and hold it against the band.

Then take a crystal, thread it onto the wire and take it back down through the hole in the flower. Gently ease the wire so the bead holds the flower tightly against the band then wrap the wire around the top of the hair comb behind the shell to secure.

Repeat this process twice more with each flower.

3

If you feel the flowers need to be more secure simply put a dab of glue on the back of the petals where they touch the band.

tahitian shell hair comb

If you ever longed to be on a luxurious holiday involving lots of sun and sand on a South Pacific Paradise but have never quite got there, then this comb is the one for you. Made with Tahitian shells, this accessory brings a touch of the exotic into everyday life without having to travel thousands of miles. You'll feel good, look great and you won't believe how easy it is to make.

YOU WILL NEED

MATERIALS

A gold tone hair comb measuring approx. 8cm

3 x 30mm Tahitian shell flowers

3 x 4mm light rose round Swarovski crystals

0.4mm gold plated wire

TOOLS

Round nose pliers

Flat nose pliers

Wire cutters

Strong glue (optional)

touch of coral tiara

M ade with parchment roses, this tiara has the same power as the flower of love itself. Everyone knows a thornless rose means "love at first sight" but did you know that a light salmon-pink rose – just like the ones used in our tiara – means the wearer will have a brilliant complexion, a glowing smile and enjoy perfect happiness? OK, so we can't promise you all these attributes just by wearing the 'Touch of Coral' tiara but the way this accessory will make you look and feel, we can practically guarantee you'll radiate a brilliant and glowing happiness.

step-by-step

YOU WILL NEED

MATERIALS

1 silver tone tiara band

0.4mm silver plated wire

11 x salmon pink and white parchment tea roses (with attached wire)

6 x white parchment tea roses (with attached wire)

10 x 6mm Swarovski white pearls

4 x 6mm light rose Swarovski round crystals

4 x 5mm clear Swarovski round crystals

2 x silver tone metal leaves (with attached wire)

1m x 6mm peach satin ribbon (optional)

TOOLS

Wire cutters

Round nose pliers

Flat nose pliers

Strong glue

Position 10 salmon pink and white tea roses centrally on the tiara band. Take a rose and hold it in place on the front of the band, then wrap the wire around the band a few times so it is fixed.

Take the next rose and position it snugly against the first. Hold it in place and, just like the first rose, wrap the wire behind.

Continue until 10 roses are fixed along the band. Neaten off any excess wire.

Now create an arc of 6 white roses. Push the wire of each rose so it is at right angles to the back of the rose head.

Take the first two roses and place the heads together so the wires are in opposite directions to each other. Twist one wire once around the other so they are fixed together.

79

3

4

Now build on this with the next rose and secure the wire behind by wrapping it around the existing wires. Continue until there are six roses in a line. Mould these into an arc shape with your fingers.

Fix the remaining salmon and white rose to the centre of the arc (between the third and fourth rose) by bending the wire to a right angle and wrapping it around the wires in the arc.

Now place the whole arc over the salmon and white roses on the headband and fix each end between the third and fourth rose and seventh and eighth rose respectively by wrapping the wires around the band.

5

Create two sprays of four pearls each (see numbers 6 and 7 in Techniques section) and wire wrap them to the back of the band so they fill the space below the arc.

Now create two more sprays. Using the wire already attached to a silver leaf, incorporate it into a spray with 1 pearl, 2 rose pink crystals and 2 clear crystals (see numbers 6 and 7 in Techniques section).

Repeat so you have a similar spray for each side.

Attach the first spray to the band between the first and second salmon and white roses and the second spray between the ninth and tenth roses.

After wrapping the wire, neaten off all ends and press them securely into the band so no sharp points stick out.

The next part is optional but in my opinion does tend to give a 'finished' look to the whole accessory. Wrap the ends of the tiara band with peach ribbon starting from the edge of the roses.

Glue one end of ribbon to the back of the band just behind the last rose and wrap around the band so the edges of ribbon just overlap each other. Continue wrapping until you reach the end of the tiara. Make sure there are no gaps and secure with a dab of glue.

Repeat the process on the other side.

step-by-step

1

Starting at one end of the comb, take a length of wire as long as you can comfortably manage, probably about 50cm, and attach it by wrapping it a few times around the top. Then continue by making bead twists and clusters in both AB clear and light amethyst bicones (see number 6 and 7 in Techniques section) across the top of the hair comb.

2

Vary the heights and make up of the twists, using one, two or three beads.

3

Now, take the parchment roses and push the wire of each rose so it is at right angles to the back of the rose head.

Again, starting at one end, place a rose head on the front of the comb and wrap the wire around the band to make it secure.

Cut off any excess wire and flatten the remaining wire to the band with flat nose pliers.

4

Continue to work your way across the whole length of the comb, fitting each rose snugly against the last one and neatening off the wires each time you wrap.

roses & crystal hair comb

If you think a full tiara like 'a Touch of Coral' is perhaps too formal looking or over the top for a certain occasion, then this comb could provide the answer. As you can see, parchment roses are extremely versatile when making hair accessories – on this comb, the base is adorned with roses while the abundance of crystal above makes the light shimmer and dance, highlighting the gentle lilac hues.

YOU WILL NEED

MATERIALS
1 gold tone hair comb approx. 8cm long

0.4mm gold plated wire

8 x lilac and white parchment tea roses (with attached wire)

25 x 4mm AB clear Swarovski bicones

26 x 4mm light amethyst Swarovski bicones

TOOLS
Wire cutters

Round nose pliers

Flat nose pliers

eternity clip

T he Eternity clip is a statement of discreet elegance that attracts the desired attention without shouting about it. Reminiscent of the symbol for infinity, this piece delicately yet firmly announces a star has arrived.

YOU WILL NEED

MATERIALS
Silver tone bar clip (approx. 5.5cm long)

0.6mm silver plated wire x 30cm (approx.)

3 x 6mm AB clear round Swarovski cabochons

14 x 4mm light green Swarovski bicones

10 x 3mm peridot Swarovski flatbacks

TOOLS
Wire cutters

Flat nose pliers

Tape measure

Strong glue

step-by-step

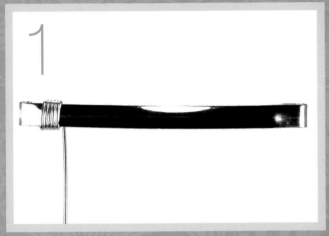

1 Take the front of the clip and anchor the wire to one end by wrapping it around five or six times. This is so a base will be made that is large enough to hold a cabochon.

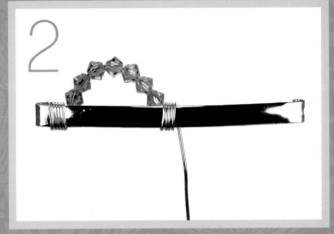

2 Measure and mark the centre of the clip then thread 7 bicones onto the wire. Allow the wire with the beads to form an arc and again wrap the wire a few times around the middle of the clip so a base, large enough to hold a cabochon, is formed. Wrap the wire so the end leaves the clip on the opposite side to the beads.

3 Thread on the other 7 bicones and again make an arc with the beads and wire before securing it at the other end by wrapping it around the clip five more times.

4 Glue a cabochon onto each wire wrap and then secure five green flatbacks on each side of the middle cabochon. Leave to dry completely.

PROJECT 20

mini flower comb

For times when you need more than just a clip but not a full-blown hair comb – this mini comb might just do the trick. It's eye-catching and stunning but is so neat, you just can't help but fall in love with it.

This comb is perfect for yourself or perhaps for bridesmaids and flowergirls as a smaller accessory to complement the bride.

YOU WILL NEED

MATERIALS

A silver tone hair comb measuring approx. 3cm

5 x 0.8mm AB clear olive shaped Swarovski crystals

5 x size 11 clear seed beads

9 x 4mm fuchsia round Swarovski crystals

0.6mm silver plated wire (approx. 40cms)

Silver tone beading wire

TOOLS

Round nose pliers

Flat nose pliers

Wire cutters

step-by-step

1 Cut 20cms of 0.6mm wire. Measure approx. 3cms along the wire and thread a round fuchsia bead to this point. Make a wire twist (see number 6 in Techniques section).

This twist is a little tougher to make as the wire is thicker but, if you persevere, it gives a wonderful, substantial wire twist.

Attach this to the middle of the comb with a single wire wrap so the rest of the wire points downwards.

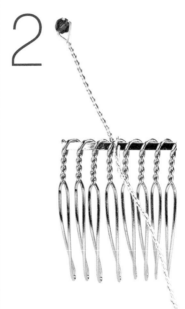

2 With the wire that is pointing downwards, make another bead twist with a three bead cluster (see numbers 6 and 7 in Techniques section) so it measures about 5cm. Neaten off the end with wire cutters and press it into the band with flat nose pliers.

step-by-step

3

Repeat this process for the other side so you have the wires crossing on the hair comb.

4

Now, using the beading wire, create the flower. Thread an olive shaped bead followed by a seed bead, then take the wire back through the olive bead. Twist the wires at the bottom to secure.

5

Repeat this process for the other four petals. Bring the end of the wire round to the base of the first petal and again twist the wires so a flower shape is made.

6

Now thread a fuchsia bead onto the wire and arrange it in the centre of the flower.

7

Attach this to the middle of the comb where the original wires cross, by wrapping the beading wire around the band and flower. Cut the end with wire cutters and press the wire close to the comb with flat nose pliers so no sharp ends stick out.

list of suppliers

P. J. Beads
583C Liverpool Rd
Ainsdale
Southport PR8 3LU
United Kingdom
Tel: +44 (0)1704 575461
Fax: +44 (0)1704 576181
Website: www.beads.co.uk
Email: jewelry@beads.co.uk

TiaraMaking.com
Suite 4
Heatley Chambers
Heatley Street
Preston
PR1 2XB
Tel: 01772 556554
Website: www.tiaramaking.com
Email:info@tiaramaking.com

Crystal-Beads.co.uk
44, Round Hill Wharf
Kidderminster
Worcestershire
DY11 6US
Website: www.crystal-beads.co.uk
Email: sales@crystal-beads.co.uk

Jewel Mania Ltd
Unit 14
Gemini Project
Landmann Way
Deptford
London
SE14 5RL
Tel: 0207 7402 143 (UK)
+44 207 7402 143 (International)
Website: www.jewelmania.co.uk
Email: sales@jewelmania.co.uk

The Bead Shop

27 Brigantine Street
Arts and Industry Estate
Byron Bay
Australia
Tel: 02 6685 8994
Fax: 02 6685 8440
Website: www.thebeadshop.com
Email: beads@thebeadshop.com

Fire Mountain Gems

1 Fire Mountain Way
Grants Pass
OR. 97526-2373
USA
Tel: 1-541-956-7891 (International)
Website: www.firemountaingems.com

Out on a Whim

121 E. Cotati Avenue
Cotati
Ca 94931
USA
Tel: 707-664-8343
Website: www.whimbeads.com

Stormcloud Trading Co

725 Snelling Avenue North
St. Paul
MN 55104
Website: www.beadstorm.com
Email: customerservice@beadstorm.com

glossary

Barrette	Ornamental bar with a pin and clasp mounted on the back
Bicone bead	The shape of a bead made by joining two cones at their bases
Cats eye bead	A bead which refracts light reminiscent of a cats eye
Seed bead	Mass produced tiny glass or plastic beads
Spacer bead	A round shaped bead usually used as a decorative element in jewellery
Bell caps	A finding used to convert a bead with no hole into a pendant using glue
Cabochon	A highly polished convex-cut but unfaceted gem
Chaton	An imitation gem backed with metal foil or silver to reflect light.
Head pins	A pin with a metal stop (head) to prevent a bead from slipping off the end
Jump ring	A plain wire ring where the ends of the wire are not soldered
Slider bead	A two or more holed bead.

index